Conceived and produced by
Lionheart Books
10 Chelmsford Square
London NW10 3AR

Editor: Lionel Bender
Designer: Ben White
Assistant Editor: Madeleine Samuel

Adapted and published in the United States in 1989 by
Hampstead Press, 387 Park Ave. South, New York NY
10016

Printed and bound in Belgium by Proost International
Book Production

Graham. Ian. 1953–
    Communications/Ian Graham.
        p.   cm. — (Science frontiers)
    Includes index.
    Summary: Examines the many forms of modern
communications, including global networks, chip developments, lasers and holograms, computers, remote
sensors, video, and future technological developments.
    ISBN 0−531−19508−2
    1. Communication — Juvenile literature.
2. Telecommunication — Juvenile literature.
[1. Communication. 2. Telecommunication.] I. Tit-
le. II. Series.
P91.2.G7 1989
001.51−dc 19   88−26025
                                                      CIP
                                                      AC

Illustrations by Hayward Art Group,
except pages 16−17, 24−25, 32−33 and 40−41,
by James G. Robins

Make up:Radius

Picture credits
Pages as numbered. T=top, B=bottom, C=center,
L=left, R=right.
5: ZEFA, 6: New Scientist/Peter Addis, 8: Science Photo
Library/Peter Aprahamian, 9: ZEFA, 10: British Telecom
International, 11T,C,B: A Shell Photograph, 12T: Inmos
Limited, 13C,B: Science Photo Library/Hank Morgan,
14: The Post Office, 15T: Associated Press, 18T: New
Scientist, 18B: Science Photo Library/John Walsh,
19T,C: Jerry Mason/New Scientist, 19B: Science Photo
Library/Hank Morgan, 20T: NASA/United Technologies,
20B: Science Photo Library/Lawrence Migdale, 21T,B:
ZEFA, 22C: ZEFA, 22B: US Geological Survey, 23TL:
Science Photo Library/Larry Mulverhill, 23TR: Science
Photo Library/NOAA, 23C: Science Photo Library/Hank
Morgan, 26T: Epson UK, 26B: ND Comtec, 27: BPCC/
Hazell Watson and Viney, 28T: Inmarsat, 28B: Science
Photo Library/Lawrence Migdale, 29T: Mullard, 29B: P.
Wallace/SERC, 30T: Science Photo Library/David Par-
ker, 30B: BT International, 31T: Mattel Games, 31B:
Sanyo, 34T,B: Canon (UK) Ltd, 35: Kodak, 36T: Associ-
ated Press, 36B: ZEFA, 37T: Science Photo Library/
Sinclair Stammers, 38L,R: New Scientist 39TL, TR:
Oxford Scientific Films/Stills, 39BL,BC,BR: Grove Park
Studio Animations, London, 42: Science Photo Library/
George Hayling, 43: Armagh Planetarium. Cover: British
Telecom International.

Cover photo: Dish-antennas at a communications
earth station.

Photo opposite: The control room at a TV
broadcasting center.

SCIENCE FRONTIERS
Communications

IAN GRAHAM

Hampstead Press New York 1989

ABOUT THIS BOOK

Science Frontiers reviews present day scientific research and development in the major areas of technology. It shows what scientists, inventors, designers and engineers are trying to achieve and why their work is essential. Why, for example, in Communications should telephone companies be replacing underground electrical cables with thin strands of glass? Why should dentists be interested in a way of making pictures with a laser? And why should movie-makers be using the world's most powerful computers?

This book is divided into four sections—Wired Society, Data Handling, The Media, and Sound and Vision. Each section describes the general trends in its area of communications technology, and then looks at specific stories of research and development. These stories are illustrated with photographs and diagrams. The last part of each section highlights the commercial spin-offs of this work and shows how familiar settings such as major sports events are likely to look in the year 2001.

At the end of the book, What Next? looks a little beyond 2001. The Glossary provides definitions of technical words used in the book.

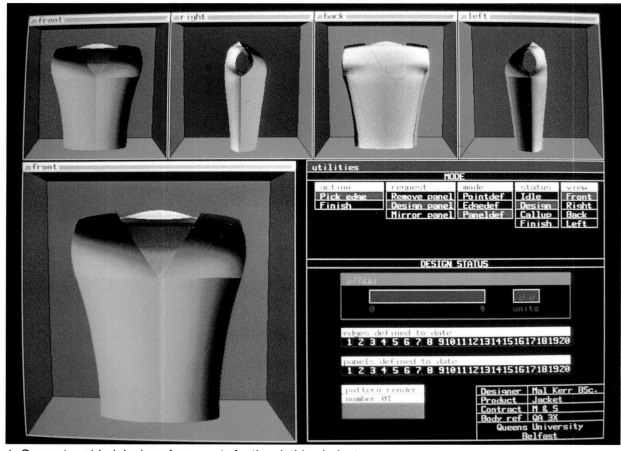

△ Computer-aided design of garments for the clothing industry.

CONTENTS

INTRODUCTION

The way we communicate with each other now is the result of research and developments in computer technology, microelectronics and space research in the last 25 years. During that time, the radio valve has been replaced by the transistor and, in turn, the transistor was replaced by the integrated circuit or silicon chip. As "chip" manufacturing technology has improved, more and more individual electronic components have been packed into the same size of chip. The latest chips contain the equivalent of several rooms full of valve-based equipment.

Advances in space research enable messages to be relayed around the world by satellite. The Earth is now encircled by dozens of satellites that provide invaluable information-gathering and communications services to weather forecasters, geologists, telephone companies, television broadcasters and many others. Research and development in laser technology is continually producing new uses for lasers, especially in communications and information storage.

The following pages present a selection of the latest ideas, designs and inventions created as solutions for today's technological problems.

▽ In education, computers are being used more and more to develop language and creative skills as well as logical thinking.

▷ Communications antennas are taking on weird forms and attachments as they handle an increasing range of signals.

WORLDWIDE NETWORKS

We now send more information farther and faster than ever before. Telephone conversations, television and radio programs, computer data and printed text are transmitted around the world and also into space. Satellites orbiting the Earth receive signals from transmitters on the ground and then relay them back to Earth. Satellite transmissions suffer much less from the problems of radio transmission which can be distorted or blocked altogether by hills, tall buildings, and peculiar weather conditions. A single satellite can relay signals to an entire continent. Computers control these communications systems. The cost of processing information by computer is falling, and computer-operating speeds are increasing. In future, communications systems will continue to transmit information faster and more cheaply.

▽ The Madeley earth station in England is a vital link in Britain's communications with the rest of the world. Its dish antennas connect Britain by satellite with over 80 countries, 24 hours a day.

⦿ MESSAGES ON THE MOVE

Every day people thousands of miles apart in different countries speak to each other by telephone as if they were neighbors. Most of these telephone calls are relayed around the world by communications satellites. Earth stations link these satellites with each nation's telephone network. The Earth station's dish-shaped antennas each point at a satellite orbiting 35,800 km (22,300 mi) above the equator. This exact height is chosen because a satellite in this orbit moves around the Earth at the same speed as the Earth spins. The satellite therefore always stays over the same point on the ground.

Satellites are being made bigger and more powerful all the time. Early Bird, one of the first communications satellites launched in the 1960s, could relay 240 telephone calls simultaneously across the Atlantic Ocean. Satellites now in orbit can relay tens of thousands of telephone calls along with a couple of television channels. Many satellites carry other forms of communication such as telex messages and computer data.

▼ REAL-TIME SITUATIONS

Worldwide communications networks allow people to respond to changing situations as they happen—in real time, as it is called. In the oil industry, refineries located on the coast make gasoline and other fuel from crude oil. The crude oil is delivered to refineries from oil fields all over the world by tanker ships. An increase in the price of crude oil may reduce demand. Political changes in countries that control oil fields can affect the availability of crude oil.

△ Computerized fuel pumps and credit card registers provide oil companies with information about sales.

▽ Satellites orbiting the Earth provide voice and computer data links between oil tankers and the oil rigs and refineries that they sail between.

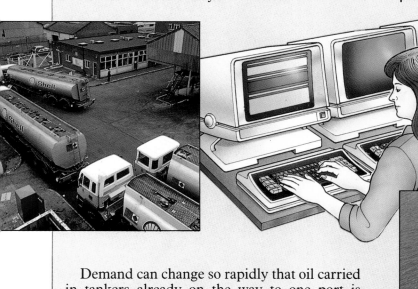

Demand can change so rapidly that oil carried in tankers already on the way to one port is needed more urgently somewhere else. Computerized registers in filling stations relay sales information to oil companies. Using computers, the companies can then identify trends in sales and detect sudden changes in the marketplace the moment they happen. Refinery output is matched to changing demand. Oil tankers at sea can be directed to change course and head for a different port, so that oil is always sent to where it is needed most.

CHIP DEVELOPMENTS

In the 1990s some computerized machinery will possibly "see," "hear" and "talk." Making a computer speak is not difficult. However, it is very difficult to make a computer understand speech. That is because people speak in different languages, with different accents and at different speeds. Languages have rules which can be programmed into a computer, but people do not always follow the rules. Computerized voice-recognition systems are now in use, but before they can function they have to learn the sound of the operator's voice. In addition, the operator can use only the limited number of words stored in the computer's memory. New types of chips (computer circuits) and new ways of building computers might someday enable computers to do these traditionally human jobs efficiently.

▶ PARALLEL PROCESSING

Today's computers do not work quickly enough to handle the jobs they will have to do in the next decade. Speech synthesis, voice recognition and robot vision require large amounts of information to be processed very rapidly. Computers built with new chips bearing hundreds of thousands of electronic components will provide the processing power that future systems need. Such a system involves a problem by dividing it up into lots of smaller parts. Each chip works on a different part of the problem and all of them

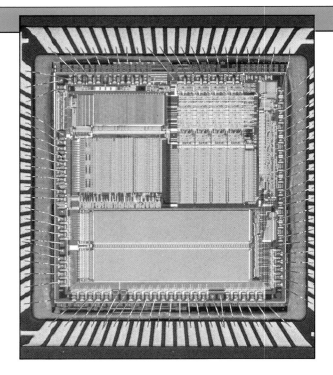

△ The transputer is a new type of computer chip to be used for parallel processing. Each 9 mm-sq chip contains 200,000 components.

work at the same time. The time taken to solve a problem is therefore greatly reduced. The system's problem-solving power can be increased by adding more chips. There will be no limit to the number of such chips that can be connected together.

◀ THE COMPUTERIZED COCKPIT

Computers are taking over more of the work involved in flying a plane. Advances in aviation electronics are changing the design of aircraft cockpits. Until the 1980s, cockpit control panels were full of dozens of instruments called gauges. Each gauge had a single function. It might show the temperature of an engine or the aircraft's speed. The cockpit of the 1990s has between two and six television screens instead of dozens of gauges. All the information that was previously shown on gauges is still collected from the aircraft, but it is now sent to a computer. If the engines and controls are working properly, the information is not shown to the pilot unless requested. If a problem occurs, the computer detects it and alerts the pilot.

◁ A prototype electronic cockpit for a U.S. fighter plane of the 1990s. Direct Voice Input systems will enable the pilot to speak flight instructions into the plane's computer.

▷ WISARD is a vision system designed as a neural network at Brunel University, England, for future use in robots. If an object is placed in front of the system's eye (a television camera) WISARD learns what it looks like. It does this by recording whether the points in a random pattern on the image are light or dark. This information is stored. Later, when a new object is placed in front of WISARD, the same points are compared with its memory until a matching pattern is found.

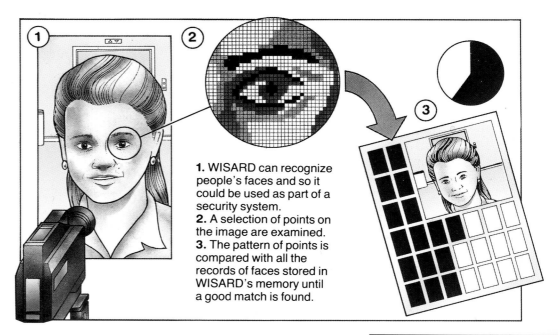

1. WISARD can recognize people's faces and so it could be used as part of a security system.
2. A selection of points on the image are examined.
3. The pattern of points is compared with all the records of faces stored in WISARD's memory until a good match is found.

Ⓐ NEURAL NETWORKS

Computers in general use today work by following very precise instructions stored in the computer's memory. If an instruction is missing or information is not given to the computer in the correct way, the program stops. People's brains work differently. We can take in information in different forms—text, pictures, spoken words, music, touch and smell. The information does not even have to be complete for us to tackle a problem and arrive at a solution. Researchers are looking for ways of building computers that process information in this way. An approach under investigation is to use electronic circuits that resemble brain cells. Each circuit component can receive and transmit signals, and connects with not just two but hundreds of neighboring components. Prototypes of these "neural networks" have been built. One, called WISARD, recognizes faces it has seen before.

Ⓑ VOICE RECOGNITION/SYNTHESIS

There are two ways of making a computer speak. In the first, words spoken into a microphone are divided up into a series of fractions of a second of sound. Each slice of a word is changed into an electrical code that is stored in the computer's memory. Later, the computer reassembles the slices in the correct order and changes them back into sound. The computer voice is realistic, but it can only speak the words it has learned. The second method is more versatile. A computer is programmed with the rules of a language and the simplest sounds that words are made from. The computer can make any word, phrase or

▷ Voice recognition systems such as this IBM experimental model could replace keyboards. The word "baby" spoken into the microphone is analyzed and identified by the computer.

sentence required, but its voice is not as lifelike as in the first method. If a computer could understand human speech it would have unlimited uses in controlling machinery. Systems now under investigation begin by dividing spoken words into the different frequencies of sound they contain. This computer compares the frequency patterns with patterns stored in its memory until a match is found.

13

Communication networks now use digital electronics. Signals no longer travel as varying waves of electrical current, but as discrete pulses. This has resulted in new communications opportunities. Telephones can now be programmed to remember numbers and redial busy numbers. Several callers can talk to each other in a teleconference, or see each other in a videoconference. The copper cables that used to carry telephone calls are being replaced with optical fibers. These are more reliable, they can carry more information down a thinner cable, and they are made from cheaper materials. Optical Character Recognition (OCR) machines read typed addresses on envelopes and code mail for electronic sorting machines.

Recording blood pressure at home using a portable monitor. The records are sent by telephone to the hospital.

▽ ELECTRONIC MAIL

Companies exchange information by telephone and by mail. A new way of communicating, called electronic mail, uses the ability of computers to communicate with each other by telephone. Most company mail is prepared by computers. The paper stage can be eliminated and the information sent from computer to computer. Electronic mail is faster than traditional mail—messages travel in seconds. Mail can be collected in a central "mailbox" (a computer's memory) similar to a sorting office, and forwarded to the addressees later. This is called store-and-forward. Alternatively, messages can be sent directly to their final addresses and dealt with immediately or stored for reading later.

◔ MEDI-CALL

In medical emergencies, information about the condition of a patient has to be collected and analyzed very rapidly. Medical specialists cannot go out with ambulances to the scene of every accident. However, the necessary information can be relayed to them at the hospital. A description of a patient's condition is sent by radio. Sensors attached to the patient collect information about electrical activity in the

▷ One of the world's fastest mail sorting machines in action. The machine decodes address information in patterns of chemical dots printed on the envelopes by an OCR machine. Using the code, it can divide up letters according to their addresses at the rate of 32,000 envelopes per hour.

patient's heart and brain. This is also transmitted by radio and appears on a screen in the hospital. It enables the staff at the hospital to advise the ambulance crew on the best form of treatment to keep the patient alive. It also helps the staff to prepare for that patient's arrival at the hospital. Consultants can be called in if necessary, equipment located and made ready, and operating-room staff alerted.

Remote medical monitoring of this type is also helpful in monitoring patients with intermittent problems, such as someone suffering from occasional heart trouble. If the heart seems to be normal when it is tested, it is difficult for doctors to decide what might be wrong. The patient carries a tiny heart monitor. When symptoms occur, the battery-powered monitor records 30 seconds of heart rhythm. The patient sends the information to the hospital by telephone.

⬇ TELE- AND VIDEO-CONFERENCING

Large companies often have offices and factories in different cities or countries. Moving people between company locations to attend conferences is expensive and wastes time. A telephone service called teleconferencing now enables distant groups of people to talk to each other as if they were in the same room. Teleconferencing can be accompanied by electronic document transfer, or facsimile transmission (fax), so that everyone can see documents being discussed. The document is fed into a fax machine that changes it into an electronic form that can be sent by telephone. A similar machine receives the information and converts it back into a printed document.

△ This TV-phone, developed by the Mitsubishi Electric Company and demonstrated at the 1987 Tokyo Communication Fair, is now available in Japan.

⬆ VIDEOPHONE

Telephone lines can carry pictures as well as sound. A screen in a sound-and-vision phone or videophone, as it is called, shows an image of the person at the other end of the line. Videophones have been demonstrated since the 1950s, but the large number of extra telephone lines needed to transmit the picture made them uneconomical to use in the home. A system developed by the Bell Telephone Laboratories in the United States in 1956 needed 125 telephone lines to form the picture. Now, using digital electronic techniques, a picture signal can be compressed so that it takes up much less space. Videophone systems are again being developed, particularly in Japan.

△ In this transatlantic videoconference, sound and pictures are relayed between France and the United States by telephone and satellite links. In New York a TV screen shows pictures of products being demonstrated in Paris. As the products and people in Paris are more mobile, two cameras are used. The choice of which picture to transmit is made by a controller, who can see the pictures from both cameras.

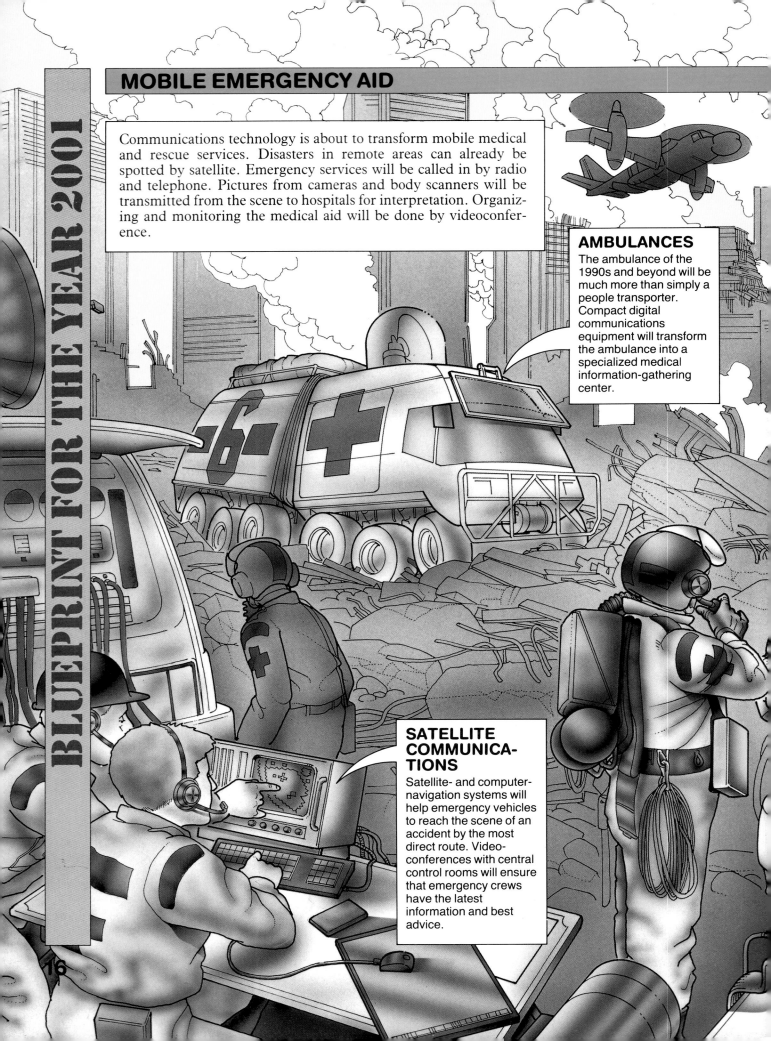

MOBILE EMERGENCY AID

Communications technology is about to transform mobile medical and rescue services. Disasters in remote areas can already be spotted by satellite. Emergency services will be called in by radio and telephone. Pictures from cameras and body scanners will be transmitted from the scene to hospitals for interpretation. Organizing and monitoring the medical aid will be done by videoconference.

AMBULANCES

The ambulance of the 1990s and beyond will be much more than simply a people transporter. Compact digital communications equipment will transform the ambulance into a specialized medical information-gathering center.

SATELLITE COMMUNICA-TIONS

Satellite- and computer-navigation systems will help emergency vehicles to reach the scene of an accident by the most direct route. Video-conferences with central control rooms will ensure that emergency crews have the latest information and best advice.

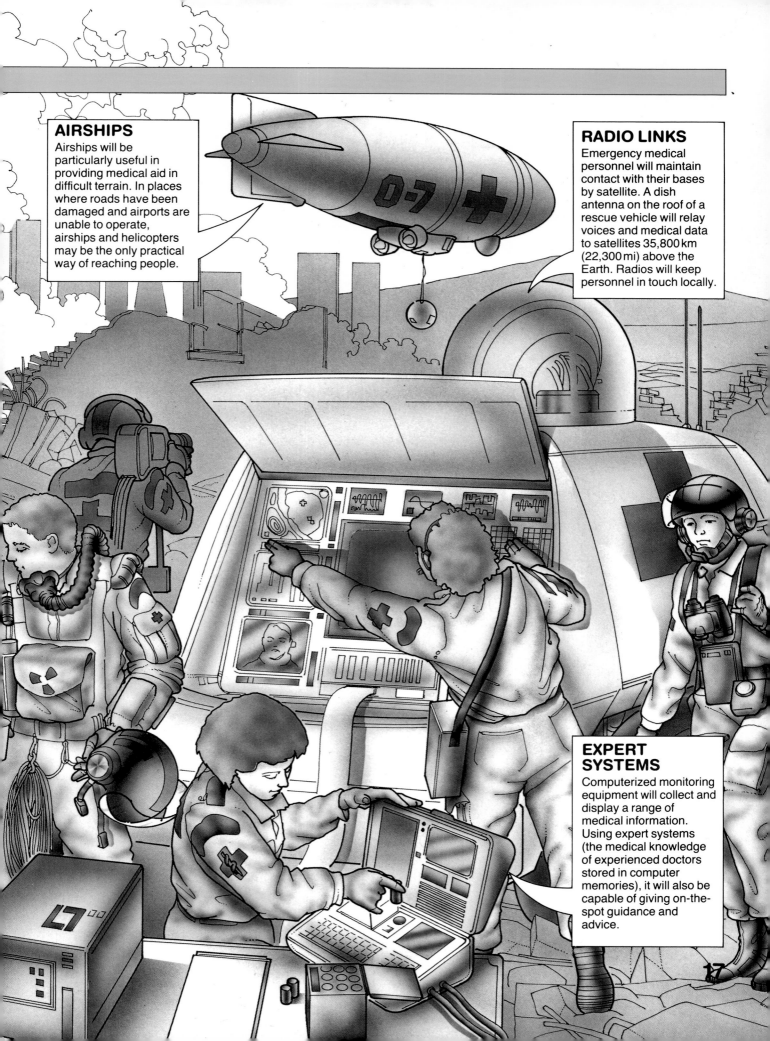

AIRSHIPS

Airships will be particularly useful in providing medical aid in difficult terrain. In places where roads have been damaged and airports are unable to operate, airships and helicopters may be the only practical way of reaching people.

RADIO LINKS

Emergency medical personnel will maintain contact with their bases by satellite. A dish antenna on the roof of a rescue vehicle will relay voices and medical data to satellites 35,800 km (22,300 mi) above the Earth. Radios will keep personnel in touch locally.

EXPERT SYSTEMS

Computerized monitoring equipment will collect and display a range of medical information. Using expert systems (the medical knowledge of experienced doctors stored in computer memories), it will also be capable of giving on-the-spot guidance and advice.

17

LASERS AND HOLOGRAMS

A laser produces a pure, intense beam of light. Depending on the type of laser, the beam may be hot enough to melt steel or delicate enough to perform surgical operations on the human eye. Lasers are used extensively in communications. GTE Laboratories in Massachusetts has transmitted 60 high-quality video programs simultaneously by laser. The beam can also carry thousands of telephone calls. Laser beams are scattered, or reflected randomly, by tiny particles in the air. This effect is used to measure the extent of air pollution or cloud cover by a technique called LIDAR—LIght Detection And Ranging—the optical equivalent of radar.

▶ SEMICONDUCTOR LASERS

Most commercial lasers are gas lasers. The beam is produced by electrically energizing gas held in a glass tube. The bulky glass tube makes the gas laser too big for many uses. Smaller lasers can be made from semiconductors, the materials that computer chips are made from. When an electric current is passed through a tiny semiconductor crystal, it produces an intense beam of invisible infrared radiation. However, this is unsuitable for uses where a visible beam is needed, such as surveying or making laser pointers. Recent Japanese research will make it possible to build more powerful semiconductor lasers with visible beams. Also, semiconductor lasers are cheaper to manufacture than gas lasers.

▶ RECORDING 3 DIMENSIONS

Lasers are used to make three-dimensional (3–D) images called holograms. Whatever angle a normal photograph is viewed from, the image appears the same. When you look at a hologram from different angles, the objects in the image change; you see different sides of the objects, as you would in real life. To make a hologram, a laser beam is split into two beams. One illuminates a photographic plate. The other is shone onto the object to be recorded. Reflections from the object fall on the photographic plate and mix with the first beam. When the place is developed and illuminated again, the object reappears. The lifelike appearance of objects in holograms is very useful. Holograms of welds in metal are studied for signs of cracks. The 3–D nature of the holograms contains much more information than a photograph. X-ray photographs of sections through the human body can be stored on a hologram, producing a 3–D image of the body with all its internal details.

△ Lasers can play music too. Interrupting the beams of this laser harp switches sound generators on and off. Each beam triggers a note.

▽ A hologram of a patient's teeth is as accurate as a plaster mold but cheaper to make.

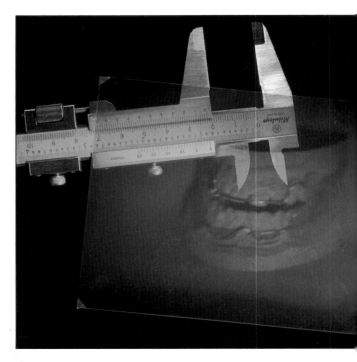

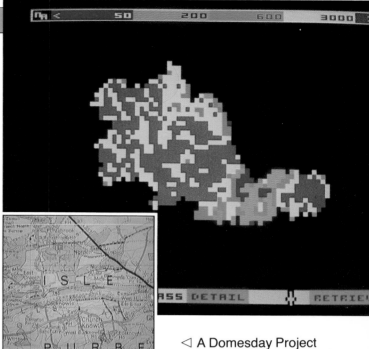

LASER COMMUNICATIONS

A beam of light can be used for communications. Using high-speed digital electronics, a laser beam can be made to flash on and off 100 million times every second. Signals switching at these speeds can carry spoken messages, computer data, and television pictures. The beams are transmitted along fine strands of glass called optical fibers. The fibers can be bent around obstacles and the light beams inside them bend too. This ensures that the maximum amount of light entering one end of the fiber reaches the receiver at the other end. The fibers are bundled together into optical cables, which are now replacing metal cables carrying electrical signals.

Optical fibers have several advantages over metal cables. They are made from a cheaper material – molten sand. They carry more information via a thinner cable. The light beams are not affected by electrical interference.

▽ Researchers at Columbia University are using optical fibers instead of wires to connect computer chips together. Light carries information between the chips much faster than the wires of a conventional computer.

◁ A Domesday Project user can zoom in on a small area the United Kingdom from space by selecting a series of satellite photographs, aerial pictures, maps of different scales, and photographs taken from ground level. Text and tables of information about the area selected can also be displayed.

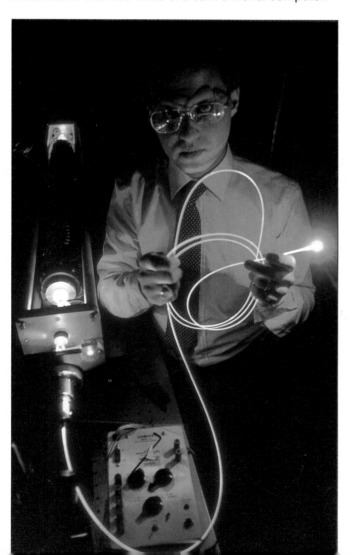

⊙ DOMESDAY PROJECT

In 1066 William the Conqueror's army invaded England from France and defeated King Harold. Twenty years later, William's officials produced a book called the Domesday Book. Its two volumes listed all the lands in the kingdom, who owned them, what other property they owned, and what the property was worth. It provided the king with the information needed for levying taxes and valuing his lands. In 1986 the BBC, Philips and Acorn Computers produced a modern Domesday book. Like the 1086 publication, it contains two volumes, but they are not books. They are laser disks. The two 30 cm (12 in) disks contain 150,000 pages of text, 74,000 pictures, 9,000 tables of statistics, moving video sequences, sounds and computer graphics. Together these give a survey of the United Kingdom and its people in the 1980s. The disks store over one million screen displays, and they are read by a laser player controlled by a computer. The user can browse through the screen displays or select any single display, just as one uses an encyclopedia.

19

NUMBER CRUNCHING

The world's most powerful computers can do over a billion calculations every second. The high computing speed of these supercomputers is necessary for such tasks as weather forecasting and police investigations. The atmosphere is a complex system, with air temperatures and pressures changing continually in different ways at different heights. Without a supercomputer, the many millions of calculations needed to analyze the data could not be done in the time available. Criminals can often be identified from fingerprints left at the scene of a crime. Matching an unknown print with one of the millions in police files is a time consuming job now being done by powerful computers.

▼ CRAY COMPUTERS

Cray Research began building supercomputers in the United States in the mid-1970s. From the start its goal was to build the world's most powerful computers. Now the majority of supercomputers used throughout the world are made by Cray. They are used mainly for scientific and engineering research where a huge number of mathematical calculations must be done in a short time. The latest model, the Cray-2, looks unlike most other computers. Its circular shape minimizes the lengths of electrical connections in the computer. This enables information to be exchanged between the various parts of the computer more quickly.

When a computer works, it produces heat. The faster it works and the smaller it is, the more heat is generates. Without a cooling system the temperature of the Cray-2 would increase until its circuits failed. The circuit boards inside the black towers are bathed in a cooling liquid that does not conduct electricity.

△ The National Aeronautics and Space Administration (NASA), is using a Cray-2 supercomputer to help design the X-30, the prototype of a new spaceplane to replace the Space Shuttle.

◁ The Cray-2 supercomputer was introduced in 1985. It has a 256-million-word memory and can do 1.72 billion calculations per second, yet it stands only 1.14 m (about 3.7 ft) high and 1.3 m (about 4.3 ft) across.

▽ PLAYING WITH PARTICLES

In physics research it is sometimes difficult or impossible to carry out experiments to test theories. Particles may be so small that they cannot be observed, or events may happen so quickly that they cannot be studied. Computers are used to simulate these events. A computer is programmed with, say, a theory of atoms that scientists wish to test. It then calculates what will happen after collisions between atoms of a known size and shape, traveling at given speeds and in certain directions. Analyses of the results, also done by computer, are used to develop the scientists' theories a little further.

Most of the chemicals in living things contain thousands of atoms. Computers are used to work out how the atoms fit together and how the chemicals combine and interact with one another. Knowing this helps medical researchers to understand how disease organisms such as the AIDS virus invade the body, or why some people are born with abnormalities. Clues gained in this way help researchers to design drugs to combat viruses and detect abnormalities before birth.

▷ SOUND SYNTHESIZING

All natural sounds are composed of many different frequencies. A computer can be programmed to simulate the particular mix of frequencies produced by any musical instrument or a human voice. First, a sample of the sound is fed into the computer from a microphone. Since the computer stores numbers only, it converts the sound into a stream of numbers. It does this by analyzing the sound perhaps 30,000 times every second and storing the frequencies present in each sample as a series of numbers. To reproduce the sound, the computer converts the numbers back into individual pulses of sound. However, the pulses are produced so rapidly that they merge together. The computer can also change the sounds by processing the numbers in its memory. It can even create entirely new sounds that cannot be made by existing musical instruments.

△ In studios like this, sounds are created, mixed together and stored in computer memories. The knobs on the mixing desks enable sound engineers to control sounds.

◁ The control room of the Canadian TRIUMF atomic-particle accelerator. An accelerator produces violent collisions between particles within an atom. The results can be analyzed only by powerful computers.

21

REMOTE SENSING

Scientists can learn a lot about an object by analyzing the radiation, such as heat, light and radio waves, coming from it. With stars and galaxies it is the *only* way of studying the object. This is called remote sensing—sensing from a distance. Remote sensing is invaluable in studying the Earth. Some of the cameras carried by Earth-orbiting satellites survey the Earth by recording visible light. Others record the normally invisible infrared, ultraviolet, and radio wavelengths. A single satellite image can provide information that would take weeks to collect on the ground at much greater expense.

▶ INFORMATION FROM SPACE

The Earth's atmosphere, lands, and oceans are monitored by satellites. Some are "geostationary," such as the Meteosat weather satellites. By orbiting at a height of 35,800 km (22,300 mi) above the equator, they stay over the same place on the Earth's surface. Others, such as the Landsat Earth resources satellites, orbit from the North Pole to the South Pole, only 800–1000 km (about 500 mi) above the surface. They

take between 90 and 100 minutes to complete each orbit. As the Earth spins beneath them, their orbits eventually take them over every part of the globe. Photographs taken by such satellites clearly reveal information that cannot easily be obtained at ground level–the location of valuable mineral reserves, the spread of crop diseases, and the course of pollution in rivers and seaways, for example. These pictures are transmitted by radio as a stream of electrical pulses to receiving stations on Earth.

△ Different types of rock reflect the Sun's energy differently. Satellite pictures are color coded by computer to show these variations and identify rock types. Even features under the surface, such as oil deposits, show up when viewed from space.

△ A patient undergoing a CAT scan. The patient lies inside the machine while the scanner rotates, taking a series of X-ray pictures that are viewed on a screen.

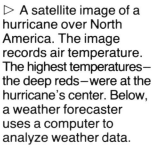

▷ A satellite image of a hurricane over North America. The image records air temperature. The highest temperatures—the deep reds—were at the hurricane's center. Below, a weather forecaster uses a computer to analyze weather data.

ⓐ SEEING INSIDE A BODY

In medicine, a variety of remote sensing techniques enable doctors to look inside the body without the need for surgery. Beams of short-wavelength radiation pass through the body's soft tissues (skin and muscle) and strike photographic film, but they are blocked by bones. This is an X-ray. If a series of X-rays are taken from different directions, a computer can convert them into a single picture of a slice through the body. The technique is called Computed Axial Tomography (*axis* is Latin for a pivot, *tome* is Greek for a slice); the picture is called a CAT scan.

In another technique, called Magnetic Resonance (MR), the patient is placed in a magnetic field of constant strength. Hydrogen atoms in the body turn, like compass needles, to lie in the same direction as the field. The body is then exposed to a pulse of a second magnetic field. The hydrogen atoms absorb enough energy from the pulse to break away from the first field. When the magnetic pulse ends, they are pulled back into the first field again. As the atoms move back, or resonate, they produce their own magnetic field. This is detected and used by computers to produce a much more detailed picture of the body's internal structure than X-rays can produce.

ⓐ FORECASTING WEATHER

Satellites enable weather forecasters to monitor the progress of weather systems as they move across large areas of the Earth. Meteosat weather satellites photograph the complete Earth disk (about a quarter of the Earth's surface) every 30 minutes. Two National Oceanic and Atmospheric Administration (NOAA) polar-orbiting satellites photograph smaller areas. The NOAA satellites also receive information transmitted from weather ships, buoys at sea and balloons ascending through the atmosphere. They relay the information to ground stations as they fly over them. Data received from the satellites are fed into computers programmed with mathematical models of the atmosphere. These models predict the speed and direction of weather systems.

The European Space Agency (ESA) is developing a new type of satellite-borne laser to help give earlier warning of hurricanes. The satellite is expected to be ready for launch into orbit by 1990. The laser will detect the wind patterns that usually develop into hurricane-force storms. They will do this by measuring the change in wavelength of laser light reflected back into space by tiny particles always present in the air. This indicates the wind speed and direction.

FIGHTING FIRE

REMOTE SENSING

Remote sensing cameras will locate survivors through smoke and debris by detecting the heat of their bodies. Lasers will plot the extent of air pollution. Satellites will monitor movements of air and water pollution. Satellites will also follow the aftereffects of pollution on large areas of vegetation over weeks or months.

PERSONNEL

Firefighters must be clearly identifiable, even when wearing breathing masks, and especially when injured and unable to speak. Holographic identification cards will contain a 3−D photograph of the holder, important medical information, and even copies of X-rays and other body scans.

The communications and information storage capabilities of lasers and holograms are only beginning to be used. Tiny lasers consuming very little power will allow small, portable equipment to make use of laser technology. Some day portable computers will be able to generate holograms from data received by radio. This will be useful for transmitting 3−D building plans and aerial views of fire to firefighters.

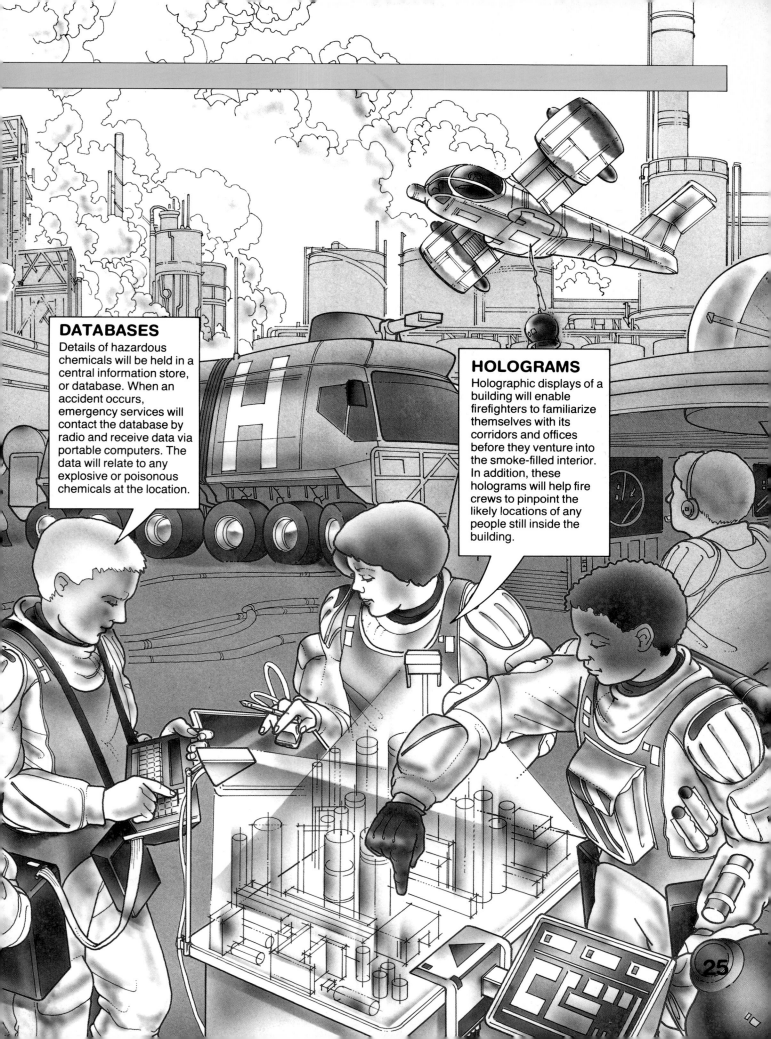

DATABASES

Details of hazardous chemicals will be held in a central information store, or database. When an accident occurs, emergency services will contact the database by radio and receive data via portable computers. The data will relate to any explosive or poisonous chemicals at the location.

HOLOGRAMS

Holographic displays of a building will enable firefighters to familiarize themselves with its corridors and offices before they venture into the smoke-filled interior. In addition, these holograms will help fire crews to pinpoint the likely locations of any people still inside the building.

25

NEWSPAPERS, PRINTING

computer

New technology has forced great changes in publishing. The word processor has taken over from the typewriter. Reporters can type stories into portable computers. The text can then be sent directly into the newspaper's computer via the telephone line. A designer displays the text and pictures on a computer screen and creates the newspaper pages electronically. The computer uses this information to make the plates from which the newspaper will be printed. Since the information can be transmitted by telephone, the printing press can be anywhere in the world.

▼ THE DIGITAL NEWSDESK

Before newspaper computers were developed, newspapers used a variety of different machines for writing and printing text. Since these machines worked in different ways, text had to be retyped each time it was passed on to another machine. Journalists now write their stories on computer terminals connected to each other and to the newspaper's central computer. In the computerized newspaper, text is typed into the computer once. After that it is passed on to editors and production staff electronically. Time is also saved in checking and researching stories.

▽ Reporters and editors in a Danish newspaper office working with a computerized system.

△ A reporter sends a story from an Epson PX-8 portable computer to his newspaper. An acoustic coupler links the computer to public telephone.

▲ THE MOBILE OFFICE

As a result of the miniaturization of computers and other electronic products, most of the equipment found in the average office can be made small enough to fit into a briefcase. Computers, printers and radiotelephones also consume much less power nowadays, so they can be powered by batteries. A typical battery-powered word processor can store approximately 200 pages of text. Linking it to a telephone

line enables the user to send the text to another telephone anywhere in the world. The briefcase system includes an acoustic coupler, which converts computer data into telephone signals. Company sales representatives frequently carry these portable computers to store details of stocks and prices and to make on-the-spot estimates for a customer.)

▼ PRINTING PRESSES

Ten years ago there were very few color photographs in newspapers. Today, they are common. New printing technology has reduced the time needed to produce publications in color from a week to several hours. As pictures are now stored electronically and not on photographic film, they can be fed instantly into the computerized page-design system. The next development is to use the same computer to control the laser that etches the printing plates. Press manufacturers are experimenting with plastic printing plates. The plastic must be sturdy enough to print a good quality image as many times as the usual, but more expensive, aluminum plate. It must also be able to print clearly on the cheaper grade papers used by the newspaper industry. The latest presses can print 70,000 newspapers an hour.)

▽ Books, such as *Science Frontiers*, are printed on modern color printing presses such as these. As with newspaper and magazine printing presses, they are becoming increasingly computerized and automated.

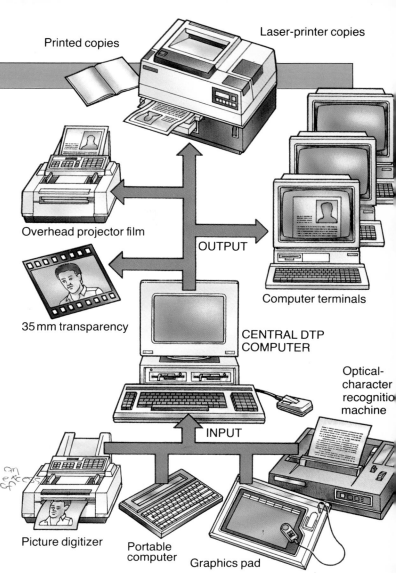

Printed copies

Laser-printer copies

Overhead projector film

OUTPUT

35 mm transparency

Computer terminals

CENTRAL DTP COMPUTER

Optical-character recognition machine

INPUT

Picture digitizer

Portable computer

Graphics pad

⦿ DESKTOP PUBLISHING

Traditional publishing usually requires expensive machines and skilled editors, designers, artists and printers. A new type of publishing using a standard office computer enables one single person to publish brochures, newsletters and magazines relatively inexpensively. The system has become known as Desktop Publishing, or DTP, because the computers and printers used are small enough to sit on a desk. Text typed into the computer is processed by the DTP program. This enables the publisher to design the pages on the computer screen. When the publisher is happy with the design, the finished pages are printed on paper by a high quality laser printer. This is desktop publishing in its simplest form. More sophisticated DTP systems have facilities for including photographs and computer graphics in the document. Text from other computers can also be fed into the system. Companies using desktop publishing systems can produce their own publications in a fraction of the time the traditional process would have taken, and at a fraction of the cost. Also, the company has more control over the production processes.

x

27

RADIO AND RADAR

Poor radio reception should be a thing of the past when Radio Data System (RDS) is introduced in the early 1990s. An RDS radio searches for a broadcast station's strongest signal and locks onto it. The station may broadcast on different frequencies in different areas of the country. As motorists drive along, their RDS radios will automatically and instantaneously be retuned.

Military radios are now so small that a soldier with a hand-held radio can communicate with headquarters from the battlefield through a sophisticated radio, data and telephone network. Some military radios can hop from one frequency to another at great speed and automatically code and decode messages to prevent the enemy from listening in.

Radio telescopes collect and analyze radio energy arriving from objects in space. They can produce detailed images of these objects even if they are hidden by interstellar dust clouds.

△ At Iberaki communications station in Japan, radio antennas, mounted on a tower, are positioned alongside a radio and television dish antenna. The antennas constantly scan the skies.

◉ EXPLOITING THE AIRWAVES

Radio waves are used to carry a wide range of information. All national and international communications systems involve radio links at some stage. Spacecraft millions of miles away in deep space communicate with control centers on Earth by radio. The European Space Agency (ESA) is currently developing a new radio-based communications system called Prodat. Using Earth-orbiting satellites, Prodat will provide satellite communications for all types of vehicles on the land, in the air and on the sea. Truck drivers and the crews of small boats and aircraft will be able to keep in constant touch with their base stations. To demonstrate Prodat, ESA has fitted 30 prototype terminals to such vehicles as long-distance turks and aircraft operated by Air France, Sabena, TAP, and Varig. To begin with, only two-way data communications will be possible. ESA will later upgrade the system so that all users will be able to talk to each other simultaneously.

△ The Nova "Star Wars" control room at the Laurence Livermore Laboratory in California. Laser weapons in space will be controlled by radio.

◉ NAVIGATION AND DETECTION

Radar (radio direction and ranging), developed during World War II, uses radio to locate objects too far away to be seen. Radio waves transmitted from a rotating antenna rush away into the distance at the speed of light (300,000 km or 186,300 mi per second). When the waves strike an object, some of them are reflected back and are received by the antenna.

The time between the transmission and its reflection is a measure of the distance from the antenna to the object. The direction of the object is simply the direction in which the antenna is pointing when the reflection is received. Passenger airliners navigate by using radio beacons (transmitters) located at known positions. After take-off, the plane aims for the first beacon. On reaching it, the aircraft is turned toward the next beacon and so on until it reaches its destination.

● BATTLEFIELD COMMUNICATIONS

Maintaining good-quality radio contact between military forces and stopping the enemy from receiving the same information is just as important as any action on the battlefield. If a signal from a transmitter can be received, the position of the transmitter, and therefore of the soldier using it, can be deduced. To help avoid detection, transmitters now being issued to troops change signal frequency many times a second, and there are up to 3,500 different frequencies to choose from. A code in the transmitted signal selected by the operator makes the radio receiver change frequency in the same way. The system automatically avoids using frequencies that are already being used by other radios.

Another way to avoid detection relies on the fact that radio location equipment needs time to work out the position of a transmitter. Some military radios store messages and then transmit them in a very short burst. The enemy, it is hoped, will not have enough time to locate them.

◁ Future wars will be fast-moving conflicts, and good radio communications will be essential to maintain an effective fighting force. Military radio systems will be smaller and lighter and feature increased security.

● MESSAGES FROM SPACE

Clouds of gas and dust in space are so dense in places that they blot out light from the stars behind them. These areas of the sky are of interest to astronomers because they can reveal information about how stars are formed. Light cannot escape from the clouds, but radio energy can. Telescopes designed to receive these radio signals can produce detailed images of the otherwise invisible stars. Computers are used to color-code the image in one of several ways. Different colors may represent different temperatures, or different materials, or how fast particles are moving, or the intensity of radiation in different places. A single color-coded image can reveal more information and can be understood more quickly than a lengthy written description of the same object.

Certain radio wavelengths are reserved for radio astronomy. No one on Earth is allowed to broadcast on these wavelengths, for that would drown the weak signals the telescope is trying to receive. Even so, radio interference from cities is still a major problem. In autumn 1987 the Indian government approved plans to build what will be the world's largest and most sensitive radio telescope. The telescope will consist of 34 separate antennas spread along an arc of 25 km (about 15 mi). It is to be built in a remote part of India, far from human radio interference.

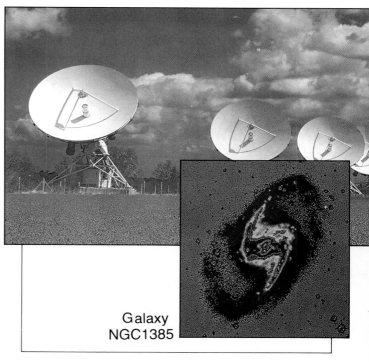

Galaxy NGC1385

△ Radio signals received by dish-shaped antennas at the Mullard Radio Astronomy Observatory in Britain produce pictures of distant objects, such as this galaxy.

THE MEDIA

TELEVISION

Television pictures and sound in the 1990s will be of a higher quality than now. A television picture is made up from hundreds of separate lines–either 525 or 625, depending on the system. Picture quality can be improved by increasing this number. New high-definition television systems produce much clearer pictures using more than 1,000 lines. Several systems have been demonstrated, but worldwide use depends on having the major broadcasting nations agree on international standards. The new television systems will also feature high-quality stereo digital sound.

▼ WORLDWIDE TV

Until the 1970s, most television programs were broadcast from land-based transmitters. Some countries with poor television reception distributed programs by cable in the worst areas. Cable television is being introduced by some countries distribute new television channels. Television stations in France and Germany receive programs by satellite from transmitters in Britain. These are received by large dish-shaped antennas and fed into the cable network linking the station with its viewers. Satellites with more powerful transmitters, such as Astra

△ One way to make satellite television profitable is to ensure that viewers pay for the programs they watch. This is done by scrambling the signals and charging viewers for a descrambler.

and Olympus 1, are being placed in orbit, enabling smaller antennas on the ground to pick up good-quality signals. In the 1990s individual homes will be able to receive television programs directly from satellites by using an 18–inch diameter dish antenna.

▽ Television programs from other countries arrive via satellite at receiving stations like this.

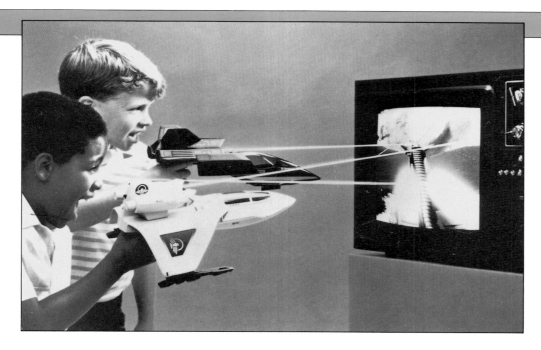

▽ Mattel's "Captain Power" game interacts with live television programs. Hand-held fighter craft fire at aircraft on the screen.

▽ New television sets and video recorders with digital image-processing facilities are capable of some special effects trickery. This Sanyo television set also uses Flatter Squarer Tube (FST) technology to create a larger picture, extending right up to the edge of the screen.

ⓐ TELEVISION GAMES

Until now, television games have been separate and different from broadcast programs. To play a television game, a cable from the games console or a home computer is plugged into the television set instead of the antenna. The set is therefore cut off from television broadcasts. The games computer generates the pictures and sound for the game. The players use hand controllers or the computer's keyboard to influence the action on the screen. Now a new type of television game is emerging. It involves using a hand controller to "shoot" at moving objects on the television screen. In a "Space Invaders" type of game the hand controller may itself be in the shape of a spacecraft or aircraft. When the player fires, the controller registers whether or not it is pointing at a target. If the player makes a hit, a point is added to the player's score. If, however, the craft on the screen fires back and the player's controller registers that it has been hit, a point is subtracted from the player's score.

ⓑ MULTISCREEN TV

The falling price of computer chips means that television sets can now make use of digital image processing. Digital television sets enable viewers to watch two or more channels at the same time. A tiny picture from one channel can be superimposed on the main picture from another channel. The tiny picture is composed of 64 lines of coded information stored in a computer memory inside the television set.

Viewers with video recorders frequently watch one channel while recording a program on a different channel. Picture-in-picture, or pip, as it has become known, allows the viewer to watch the tiny picture for

the beginning of the program to be recorded without missing any of the program being watched. The tiny picture can be moved around the screen so that it does not mask anything important on the larger picture. It may come from another television channel or it may originate from another video source altogether, such as a video camera.

BLUEPRINT FOR THE YEAR 2001

A sports event such as the Olympic Games is a major challenge to the broadcasters who televise it. Sound and pictures from all the microphones and cameras have to be routed to control rooms. Here the sound and picture to be broadcast are selected from the many options available. Several radio communications networks have to work simultaneously without causing interference to one another.

VIDEO SCREENS

Giant television screens show live action and slow motion recordings of events. Using digital video techniques, computer animation is blended with these pictures. The computer-controlled screens can show the pictures from several different video sources at the same time.

VISION CONTROL

Dozens of television cameras relay pictures of sports events to control rooms in the rim of the stadium. There, vision controllers see all the pictures on a bank of television monitors. They are also in full, two-way voice contact with their camera operators by radio.

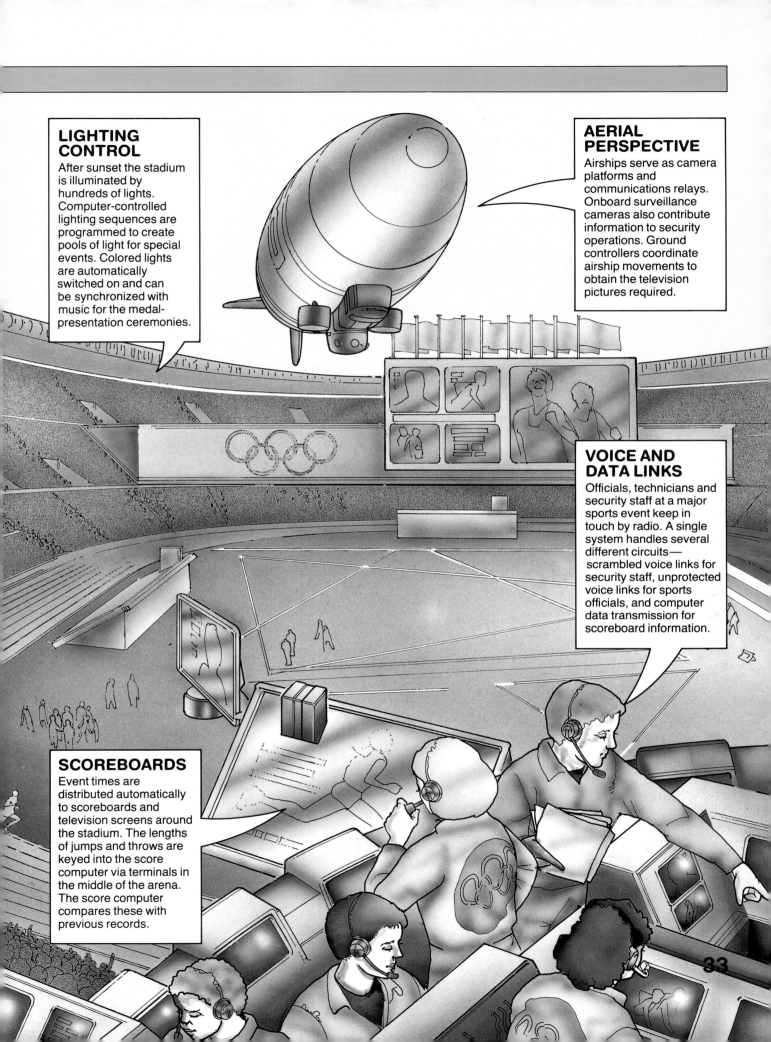

LIGHTING CONTROL

After sunset the stadium is illuminated by hundreds of lights. Computer-controlled lighting sequences are programmed to create pools of light for special events. Colored lights are automatically switched on and can be synchronized with music for the medal-presentation ceremonies.

AERIAL PERSPECTIVE

Airships serve as camera platforms and communications relays. Onboard surveillance cameras also contribute information to security operations. Ground controllers coordinate airship movements to obtain the television pictures required.

VOICE AND DATA LINKS

Officials, technicians and security staff at a major sports event keep in touch by radio. A single system handles several different circuits— scrambled voice links for security staff, unprotected voice links for sports officials, and computer data transmission for scoreboard information.

SCOREBOARDS

Event times are distributed automatically to scoreboards and television screens around the stadium. The lengths of jumps and throws are keyed into the score computer via terminals in the middle of the arena. The score computer compares these with previous records.

STILL PICTURES

There are now ways of taking photographs that did not exist 15 years ago. Images are recorded on a magnetic disk instead of on film. Data on the disk can be printed as an ordinary snapshot or converted into television pictures. A future still-picture camera might work like a video camera, making a photograph from over 1,000 screen lines. If television programs were broadcast in the same way, a home video system could take still pictures, make home videos and play prerecorded feature films. Yet continual improvements in film emulsions challenge electronics. Still photography could develop in three ways using different technologies—film, magnetic storage, and video stills.

△ Canon's Data Memory Back can transfer 16 facts about each picture to a computer.

▼ CAMERA ELECTRONICS

The availability of cheaper computer chips enables camera manufacturers to automate more camera functions. Cameras can now measure light conditions and set the shutter speed and lens aperture (lens opening) automatically. To do this, tiny electric motors are being developed for use inside cameras. Lenses for Canon's EOS camera have two banana-shaped electric motors inside every lens to operate the autofocus and aperture systems. Liquid Crystal Displays (LCDs) give data about the camera settings.

▲ COMPUTER LINKS

Still cameras use electronic circuits built from chips similar to computer chips. It is therefore very easy for cameras to communicate with computers. The new Canon T90 camera can be fitted with a Data Memory Back. Circuits in the Back store up to 16 pieces of information about 156 photographs, or 6 items about 338 photographs. In addition, the date is stored and automatically changed every day. The date, time and film frame number can be printed on the film. The Back's LCD screen can also show

◁ The EOS camera made by the Japanese manufacturer Canon is one of the most fully automated and versatile cameras available. It demonstrates future trends in 35 mm photography—chip-controlled exposure and autofocus, and liquid crystal display technology.

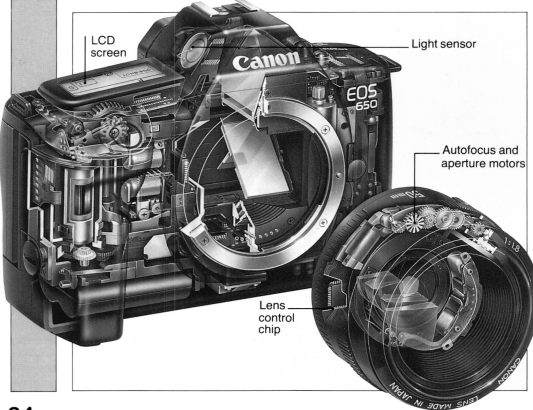

LCD screen

Light sensor

Autofocus and aperture motors

Lens control chip

information about previous exposures. The camera can be connected to a computer by cable and the information in its memory transferred to the computer's memory. It can be displayed on the computer screen and printed on paper. Comparing photographs with a list of the camera settings helps to highlight problems caused by incorrect exposure of the film. Also, in medical photography for example, it is important to know when a picture of, say, a microscope slide was taken.

▼ FILM EMULSIONS

Photographic film is now 20 million times more sensitive than the first films used in the 1820s. And improvements are still being made. More sensitive film requires less light to form an image. Therefore it can be used to take photographs under poorer light conditions without the need for a flashgun. Alternatively, in normal light it can be used with a faster shutter speed that will freeze movement and produce a sharp picture. Film emulsion—the film's light-sensitive coating—is composed of layers of silver halide crystals or grains. When the film is exposed to light, the grains are transformed into silver metal. In color film color dyes make some grains respond to only red light, others to only green and yet others to only blue.

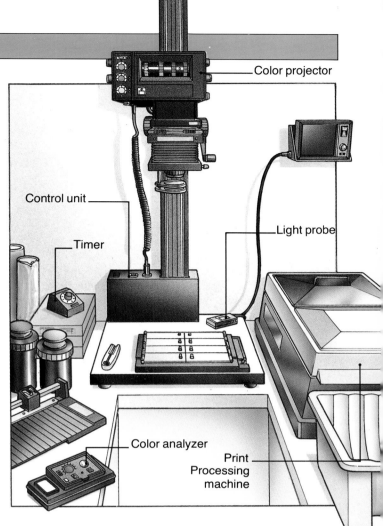

Color projector

Control unit

Timer

Light probe

Color analyzer

Print Processing machine

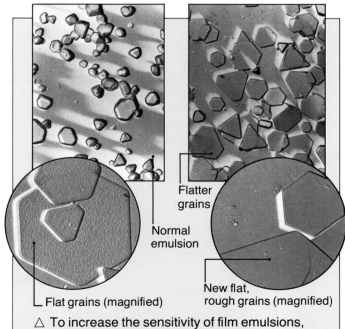

Flatter grains

Normal emulsion

New flat, rough grains (magnified)

Flat grains (magnified)

△ To increase the sensitivity of film emulsions, Kodak produced flatter silver halide grains capable of absorbing more light. By roughening the grain surface, the same size of grain can absorb twice the amount of light, giving better picture quality.

● HOME COLOR PROCESSING

Until now, few amateur photographers have attempted to make their own color prints because of the technical difficulties involved. To make a print, the film negative is placed in a photographic enlarger and the image projected onto a piece of light-sensitive printing paper for a few seconds. In one of the two forms of color printing, known as additive printing, the printing paper must be exposed three times in three different colors of light—red, green and blue. In subtractive color printing, a combination of red, yellow and blue filters produces a single light of the correct color for projecting the negative onto the paper. If any of the exposure times or filter color strengths are incorrect, the resulting print will have an all over unnatural color tint.

An enlarger such as the Durst AC707 Autocolor uses light-sensitive cells to measure the amount of each color present in the negative. A light probe is placed on the baseboard where the printing paper will later be placed. Its readings are transferred automatically to the enlarger. This enables the photographer to set the filter combination and exposure times correctly and easily. Color photos can be produced more professionally and cheaply.

VIDEO

Video recording technology developed out of the television industry's need for a way of storing programs for later transmission. Now it has spread to millions of homes. The home video recorder enables viewers to record television programs for viewing later and to watch prerecorded tapes of feature films. The future of video is closely linked with computer technology and digital electronics. Some of the latest home video recorders already use digital techniques to store a single television picture (called freeze frame) or to produce a range of other special effects. As the cost of computing power continues to fall while computing speeds increase, digital video will develop rapidly.

▶ VIDEO MONITORING

The major benefits of the video system are that it can store sound and pictures indefinitely and, since it uses television technology, the sound and pictures can be relayed to viewers anywhere in the world in only seconds. This is invaluable in education. For example, in the past, surgeons were trained by crowding around experienced surgeons at work. Very few people could stand by the operating table or watch from galleries above the table. Video has transformed this scene. Using video and satellite technology, a surgeon operating in an American teaching hospital, for instance, can demonstrate new techniques to students in India or Africa. And the tapes can be played over and over again.

▶ VIDEO CAMERAS

Recent advances in video cameras are the result of the introduction of the Charge-Coupled Device or CCD. Before CCDs, video cameras viewed objects through an image "pickup" tube. Even the best pickup tubes have disadvantages. If one is pointed at a bright light and moved, the image of the light takes seconds to disappear, causing a bright smear across the picture. An intense light may damage the tube permanently. Pickup tubes also need several seconds to warm up before they can be used and they need a very high voltage to operate. By comparison with the bulky and fragile glass pickup tube, the CCD is tiny and sturdy, and is not damaged by intense light sources. The CCD is a light-sensitive chip. Its surface is divided into over 200,000 light-sensitive spots. The image focused onto them is converted directly into an electrical signal. As CCDs are electronic devices, they do not require any warming-up before the camera can be used.

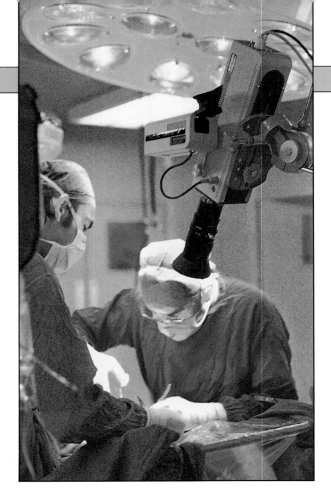

△ Particularly in teaching intricate manual skills such as surgery, video cameras are carrying clear images to very wide audiences.

▽ In Japan, Toshiba has produced a thumb-size color video camera. A pair of these tiny cameras could form the basis of future robot vision systems.

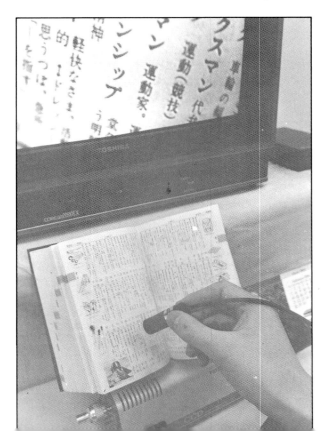

▷ Television programs are edited electronically, using machines such as these professional video tape recorders. Sequences required for the final program are selected from the original tape recordings and rerecorded onto a new video tape. The order of shots can be changed and music or sound effects can be added.

ⓐ EDITING AND IMAGE PROCESSING

The ability to edit video recordings makes it possible to produce virtually error-free programs of a precise length. It is now possible to do more than merely transfer a recording from one tape to another as in basic video editing. Pictures can be modified electronically. This image processing is done by computers. The extent of the processing is limited only by the computer program and the imagination of its operator. A computer stores pictures as numbers in its memory. Juggling the numbers changes the picture. The color or the position of different parts of the picture may be altered. Live action, cartoons, text, freehand drawings transferred directly onto the screen, and still photographs can all be mixed together. Designers of systems such as Paintbox in the United States and Quantel in the United Kingdom are constantly finding new ways of processing video images.

ⓑ VIDEO ON THE MOVE

The miniaturization of electronics has resulted in more compact video equipment. A professional video camera and recorder that 10 years ago would have filled a small room can now be carried on one shoulder. The combined video camera and recorder, called a camcorder, is now available to amateur video makers. The sound and picture quality of amateur video cameras and recorders is nearing the quality of professional recordings. Amateur video recordings of news events are now frequently broadcast in television news programs.

The way magnetic videotape is made and images are recorded on the tape has improved. The result is

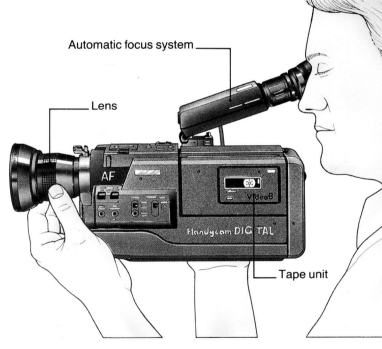

Automatic focus system

Lens

AF

Video8

Handycam DIGITAL

Tape unit

△ Video electronics are so compact that the miniaturization of video equipment is limited by the size of the tape cassette and lens. This is the Sony Video 8.

that the area of tape needed to store a single high quality television picture has decreased dramatically. The first videotape cassettes were the size of a large book. The most recent, developed for the Sony Video 8 system, are the size of a sound tape cassette.

MOTION PICTURES

Motion pictures will benefit increasingly from a wide range of new technologies. The development of computer controlled cameras enabled moviemakers to create the special effects for films such as *Star Wars*. In future, holography may be used to produce three-dimensional (3–D) films. Soviet researchers claim to have made a holographic film in full color already. The screen in a future theater may wrap around the audience. One system, designed by an Egyptian, Moheyddeen Shafik, produces a 3–D effect by placing the viewer in the middle of the action shown on the curved screen. Computers are also making a contribution to moviemaking. Their processing power can be harnessed to produce astonishingly realistic images. Full-length feature films can now be made entirely from computer generated images.

⊙ CHOOSE YOUR MOVIES
The theater of the 1990s will have the technology to ask audiences for their choice of film ending. An interactive theater was constructed for the 1986 World Fair in Vancouver, Canada. Lasers, slide projectors and film sequences shown in the theater were coordinated by computer. From time to time during the show, the theater's computer-generated voice asked questions. Members of the audience responded by pressing switches fitted to their seats. The computer analyzed the results and displayed them on the screen. When digital image processing is developed to the point where feature films can be stored in computer memory, such "interactive" theater will return.

▶ MOVIE CAMERAS
The film *Star Wars* required 365 special effects sequences to be filmed. Many of them were more complex than anything attempted before. Special effects designer John Dykstra developed a camera system to deal with the unique problems. It has become known as the Dykstraflex. The camera is mounted on a motorized crane. The electric motors that drive the crane along the floor, move its arm, and rotate the camera are linked to a computer. The camera is moved manually around a stationary spacecraft model, and its movements are stored in the computer. With the computer in control, the same movements can be repeated at different speeds, building up the shot with different models. There are other mobile, computerized cameras, but the Dykstraflex was the first capable of such precise and repeatable motion sequences and control.

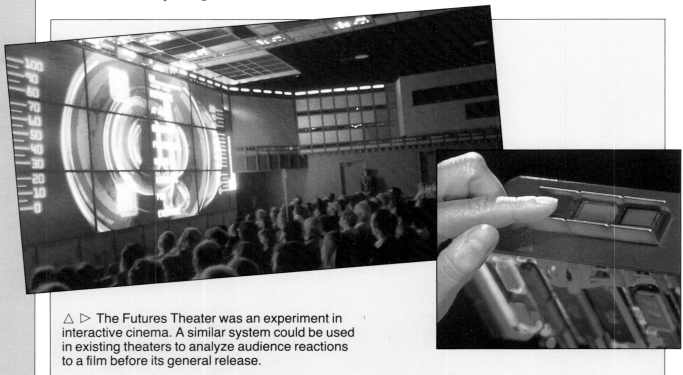

△ ▷ The Futures Theater was an experiment in interactive cinema. A similar system could be used in existing theaters to analyze audience reactions to a film before its general release.

COMPUTER-MADE FILMS

An image of an object created by an artist can be displayed on a computer screen. The computer can make the object move as if it were real. Early attempts at computer animation looked unnatural because the computers used could produce only a limited range of bright colors and blemish-free surfaces. Producing lifelike moving images of objects with subtle variations in shading, coloring and surface texture required more computing power. The company Digital Productions was the first to use a

△ Tracking a camera across a model, just above its surface, gives a realistic impression of flying. Early flight simulators worked in this way. In England, Oxford Scientific Films' Cosmoglide camera is using this principle for advertising and filmmaking effects.

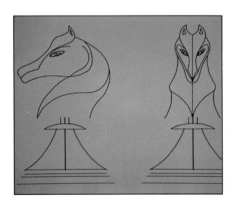 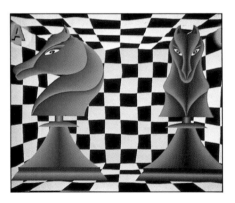 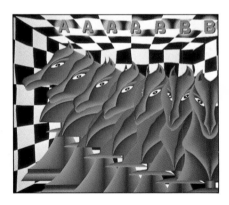

supercomputer solely for creating images. Their special-effects work for the film *The Last Starfighter* used their Cray computer for over two years.

Another computer-based technique called ray tracing promises even better realism. The computer calculates how individual rays of light from bright areas of the image would reflect from objects in the image before reaching the viewer's eye. Calculating the reflections is time consuming. Even a Cray supercomputer can take up to two hours to produce one frame of film. Cartoon animation does not suffer

△ The Antics Animation Machine was designed by animators. Given several key drawings, it will add to the drawings the necessary in-between frames and it will produce finished color images from skeleton figures.

from this problem. The movements of simpler shapes can be calculated much more swiftly. It is not necessary to generate images of every single frame of the film. Given the start and finish positions of an object or a figure, the computer fills in the frames in between. Images can also be twisted and squashed.

HOLOGRAPHIC FILM SET

Most holograms have the appearance of three-dimensional objects trapped in a flat sheet of glass. But it is also possible to create holograms that appear to hang unsupported in space in front of their flat photographic plates. At present these are little more than interesting artistic objects in holography exhibitions. In future, the creation of these space-filling holograms will find many applications, such as in movie production.

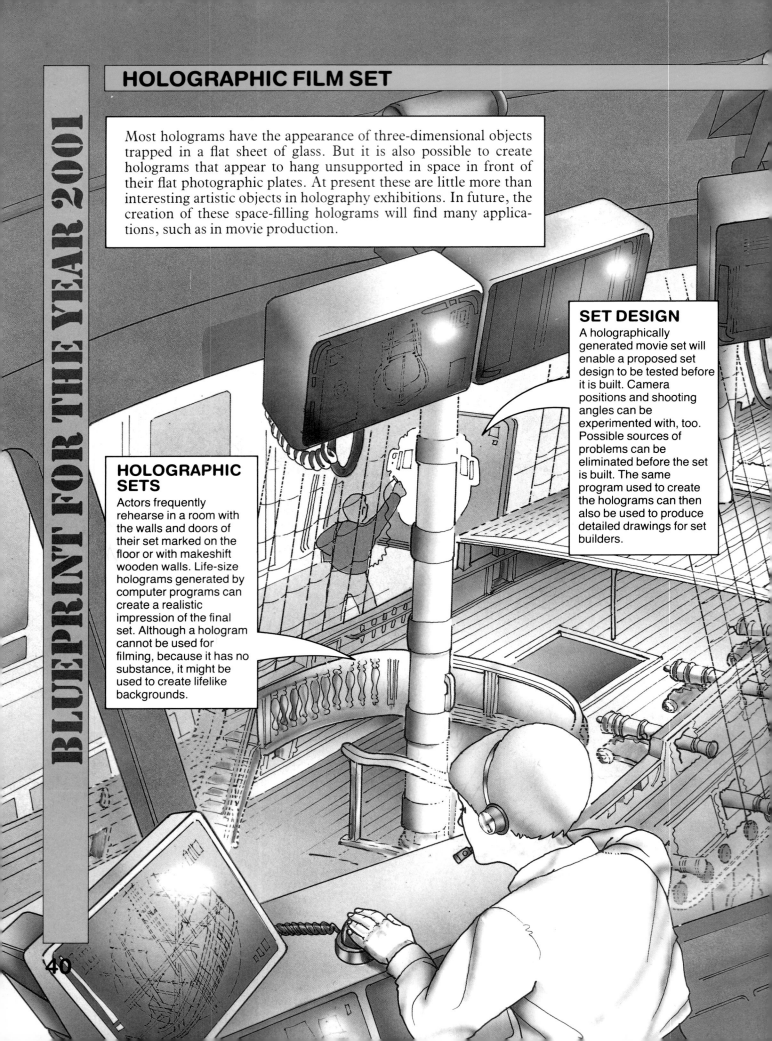

SET DESIGN

A holographically generated movie set will enable a proposed set design to be tested before it is built. Camera positions and shooting angles can be experimented with, too. Possible sources of problems can be eliminated before the set is built. The same program used to create the holograms can then also be used to produce detailed drawings for set builders.

HOLOGRAPHIC SETS

Actors frequently rehearse in a room with the walls and doors of their set marked on the floor or with makeshift wooden walls. Life-size holograms generated by computer programs can create a realistic impression of the final set. Although a hologram cannot be used for filming, because it has no substance, it might be used to create lifelike backgrounds.

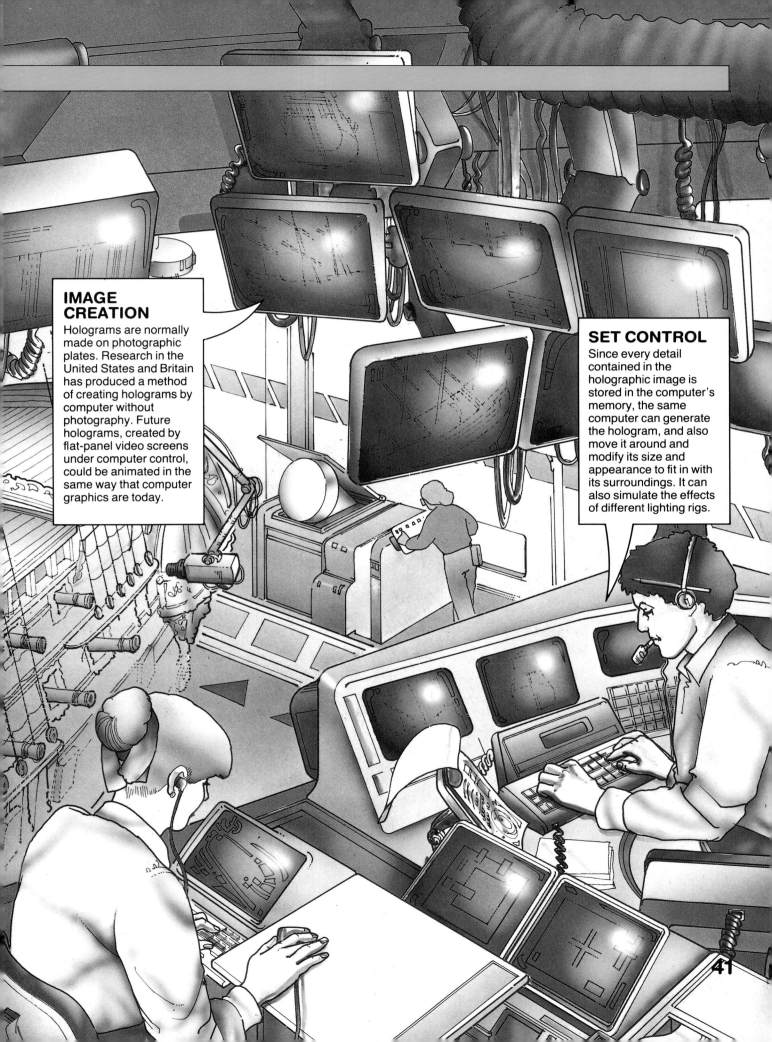

IMAGE CREATION

Holograms are normally made on photographic plates. Research in the United States and Britain has produced a method of creating holograms by computer without photography. Future holograms, created by flat-panel video screens under computer control, could be animated in the same way that computer graphics are today.

SET CONTROL

Since every detail contained in the holographic image is stored in the computer's memory, the same computer can generate the hologram, and also move it around and modify its size and appearance to fit in with its surroundings. It can also simulate the effects of different lighting rigs.

WHAT NEXT?

Many of today's technologies are still at the beginning of their development. Some, such as neural network computers, optical computers, superconductors, and visible-beam semiconductor lasers, are so new that it is difficult to speculate on how they will evolve and what kinds of applications will be found for them. The information revolution is already beginning to change people's jobs and work habits. Computing speeds will certainly continue to increase and the cost of computer power will continue to fall, resulting in more sophisticated communications systems.

▼ THE HOME WORK STATION

Videophones, flat-panel television screens, optical fiber telephone communications and faster, more powerful home computers will combine to provide the home of the future with an information center that most offices would envy today. Already, home computer hobbyists use their personal computers to achieve two-way communication with large computer databases (stores of information). In Britain, many homes receive computer data in the form of teletext transmissions. Satellite television is spreading. When the number of satellite television viewers with their own dish antennas reaches a sufficient level, it will be worth beaming other computer-based information services into the home by satellite. The means of seeing and hearing these transmissions are rather bulky now, but flat-panel television screens and flat loudspeakers will greatly reduce the space they require. In future, banking, shopping and travel booking by computer from home will be more freely available.

▽ Information handling and display technology in road vehicles is likely to follow developments in aviation. If so, today's dashboard instruments will be replaced by computer-controlled screens.

▲ ON THE MOVE

More compact communications equipment will enable cars to use radio data systems and satellite navigation. Maps displayed on a screen in the car, together with data on traffic conditions received from local radio transmitters, will enable a driver to plan the best route. In order for the driver to see the information without having to look away from the road ahead, the image may be projected onto the windshield. Displays of this type are already used in military aircraft.

◁ Increasing numbers of people are working at home in information-based jobs, called teleworking. The home information center or work station will replace the office more and more in the future.

able to "see" and recognize objects.

As robot activities become more humanlike, it becomes more difficult to devise ways of programming the computers that control them. Some robots can speak, and others have a limited ability to recognize speech. The challenge now is to bring these separate techniques and research programs together into a single robot system, the fourth-generation robot. Beyond this are "thinking" robots, the fifth generation. These will have the ability to "understand" all the information they receive and to act intelligently on it. Japan, the United States, and Britain lead the world in fifth-generation robot research.

◁ Even before an intelligent computer is developed, small mobile robots will become available for home use. The first, probably used for cleaning, will be able to avoid obstacles in their path and recharge their own batteries.

△ The school of the future may resemble the learning area in Northern Ireland's Armagh Planetarium.

⦿ INTELLIGENT ROBOTS

The machines designed to assist people are becoming more sophisticated and capable as their technology advances. The first types, or generation, of robots were little more than computer controlled mechanical arms used for paint spraying or welding in industry. The second generation of robots are able to pick up, move, and place objects down again with great accuracy. Mechanical hands looking like mechanical versions of human hands have been developed for some of these robots. The next, third generation of robots, in development now, will be

⦿ SCREEN LEARNING

The interactive nature of laser disks makes them suitable as teaching aids. On a laser disk, text, still photographs, computer graphics, sound and film can all be stored and mixed in a variety of ways. Students controlling a disk player from a computer keyboard respond to questions displayed on the screen. Depending on the answers and the way they are analyzed by the computer, the disk will jump automatically to another part of the lesson. Perhaps the player will repeat a section that has not been understood or guide a promising student through more advanced material.

GLOSSARY

Antenna The part of a radio or television system that either radiates signals away from a transmitter or collects them for a receiver.

Chip (computer) A computer circuit built on a small piece, or chip, of semiconductor material, such as silicon, about 1 cm (¼ in) square.

Digital electronics Electronic circuits that process information as a series of separate pulses representing numbers.

Facsimile transmission Also called Fax. A method of sending documents electronically. The document is converted into a series of lines of electrical information that can be transmitted by telephone.

Frequency The rate at which waves of a signal, such as a sound wave, are transmitted. It is usually given as the number of waves or cycles per second.

Geostationary orbit A special orbit around the equator. A satellite in a geostationary orbit completes one orbit in the time the Earth takes to rotate.

Hologram A three-dimensional photograph taken by laser.

Image processing Using computers to modify pictures and highlight details not normally apparent in the image.

Infrared Radiation with a wavelength longer than visible red light. Infrared radiation is therefore invisible. However, it does carry heat and so can be detected by heat sensors. See Radiation.

Interactive system A computer system designed to allow the user to control the amount and order of the information it displays. It is a two-way system.

Laser A device that produces a very pure and intense light. Pulses of laser light can be conducted along optical (glass) fibers and are used to transmit TV pictures and computer information.

Monitor (*noun*) A computer screen. (*verb*) To continually check something.

Network In communications, a network is a number of computers or, say, television transmitters, in different places, but linked together by communications channels such as cables.

Neural network A new type of computer system built to resemble the way nerves are connected together in the human brain.

Optical fibers Fine strands of glass used to carry light from lasers and thus transmitted communications signals.

Prototype The first model of something, used to test the design before it is mass produced.

Radar RAdio Direction And Ranging. A system for locating aircraft by bouncing radio waves off them and detecting the echoes.

Radiation Energy in the form of electrical and magnetic (electromagnetic) waves, including light, radio, X-rays, ultraviolet and infrared. Radiation does not need any physical medium such as air or water to travel through.

Radio telescope A telescope that collects radio waves from the sky and turns them into pictures of the stars and galaxies.

Relay A receiver and transmitter used to intercept radio signals and retransmit them, perhaps in a different direction or at a different frequency.

Robot A computer-controlled machine capable of acting on its own, without external control.

Semiconductor A material that resists the flow of an electrical current. It is neither a conductor nor an insulator. Computer chips are made from semiconductor materials such as silicon.

Simulation An artificial representation of something, usually used for research or training.

Speech recognition The identification of human speech by a computer.

Superconductor A material able to let an electric current flow through it with almost no resistance.

Teleconference A discussion among people in different places linked by communications channels. If pictures are communicated too, the discussion is called a videoconference.

Transmitter A device used to radiate radio signals away from their source.

Transputer A new type of computer chip. Many transputers can be connected together in a parallel processing computer system.

Wavelength In any wave motion such as water waves, sound waves, light or radio waves, the wavelength is the distance between any part of a wave – usually the top (crest) or bottom (trough) and the same part of the next wave.

44

INDEX

PRINTED IN BELGIUM BY

proost
INTERNATIONAL BOOK PRODUCTION